Hammerh

An Up-Close Look at the Body

by Chelsea Donaldson

Photo Credits: t = top, b = bottom, l = left, r = right, c = center

Front cover: Fred Bavendam/Minden Pictures; 1: Chris & Monique Fallows/Nature Picture Library; 2–3: Chris & Monique Fallows/Nature Picture Library; 2bl: Masa Ushioda/Stephen Frink Collection/Alamy; 2bc: Gerald Nowak/Westend61/GmbH/Alamy; 2br: blickwinkel/Schmidbauer/Alamy; 3br: Jeffrey L. Rotman/Corbis Images; 4–5: Shane Gross/Shutterstock; 4bl: Fred Bavendam/Minden Pictures; 5br: Alexander Safonov/Getty Images; 6–7: Ian Scott/Shutterstock; 7tr: David Fleetham/Nature Picture Library; 7br: Norbert Wu/Science Faction/Corbis Images; 8–9: Dan Selmeczi/Steve Bloom Images/Alamy; 10–11: Mark Conlin/Alamy; 11br: Georgette Douwma/Nature Picture Library; 12–13: Stephen Frink/Corbis Images; 12c: Mick Tsikas/Reuters; 12br: tenten10/Shutterstock; 14–15: Brandon Cole; 14cl: Jeffrey L. Rotman/Corbis Images; 14cr: Alexander Safonov/Getty Images; 15tl: Norbert Wu/Science Faction/Corbis Images; 15bc: Georgette Douwma/Nature Picture Library; 16 Ase/Shutterstock; Back Cover: Jeffrey L. Rotman/Corbis Images.

Developed and Produced by Focus Strategic Communications, Inc.
Design and Layout by Rob Scanlan
Photo Research by Karen Hunter
Photo Edit by Cynthia Carris
Illustrations by Deborah Crowle

978-0-545-75173-5

12 11 10 9 8 7 6 5 4 3 2 1   14 15 16 17 18/0

Printed in the U.S.A.   40

First printing, September 2014

Let's look at the hammerhead shark!

There are nine types of hammerhead shark.
Can you guess what they all have in common?
The odd-looking shape of their head, of course!

bonnethead

scalloped

smooth

The hammerhead shark has a wide, flat head.
It looks a little bit like a hammer . . . with eyes!
Why do you think it is shaped this way?

Let's look at the head.

This wide head helps the shark to see better.
It also helps it to hunt.
The head has many **sensors** that sense
the location of the fish.

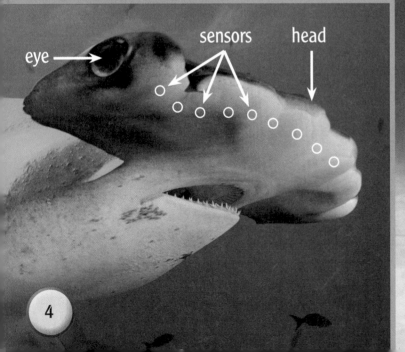

eye →

sensors   head

The shark's head has big eyes, but no nose.
So, how does the hammerhead breathe?
It uses its **gills**.

Let's look at the gills.

Gills are slits in the shark's skin.
Water passes through the gills as the shark swims.
If the shark stops swimming, it won't be able
to breathe!

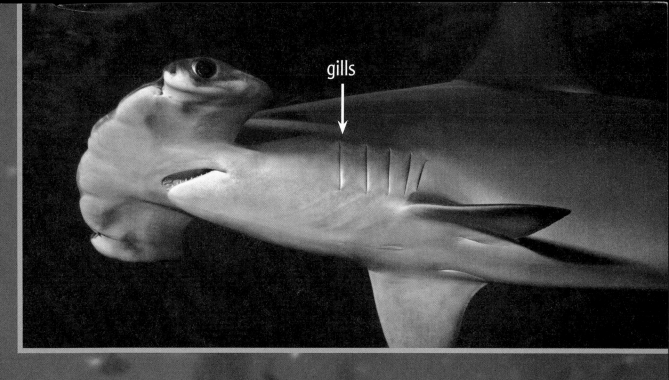

gills

Luckily, its fins and tail make swimming easy.

Let's look at the fins.

The hammerhead shark has fins on its back, sides, and underneath.
These seven fins help the shark to steer.
Its big tail helps it to move fast through the water.
It can swim about as fast as a greyhound dog can run.

tail

fin

fin

fin

fin

Do you know what else helps the hammerhead shark to swim fast?
It has a soft **skeleton** that can twist and bend!

← fin

fin

fin

Let's look at the skeleton.

Is your skeleton soft? No! It is hard and bony.
The hammerhead shark's skeleton is lighter
and more bendable than bone.
This helps the shark to float in the water.

Big Word!

cartilage (CAR-ti-lij)

The hammerhead's skeleton is made
of **cartilage**. You have cartilage, too.
You can feel it in your nose.

The hammerhead shark's teeth are not
made of bone, either.
But they are still very dangerous!

Let's look at the teeth.

11

The hammerhead has many rows of very sharp teeth.
The triangle-shaped teeth mean the shark
can saw through its **prey** in no time.
What shape are your teeth?

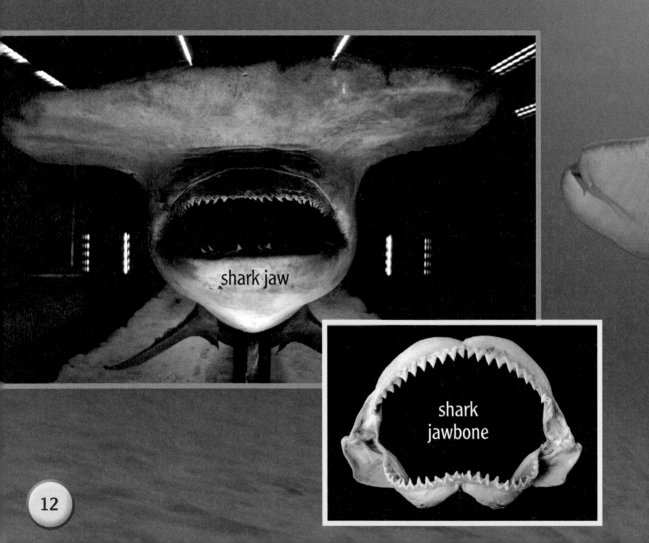

shark jaw

shark
jawbone

When the hammerhead shark loses a tooth,
a new one grows in right away.
That way, the teeth never get dull!

Who do you think has more teeth?
The hammerhead or you?

Let's look at what we have learned
about hammerhead sharks.
The hammerhead shark has:

a wide, flat head

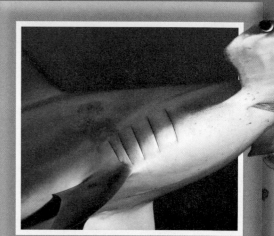

gills to help it breathe

fins and a tail for swimming

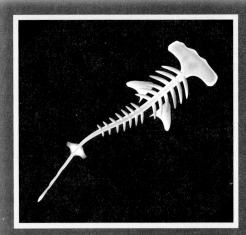

cartilage instead of bones

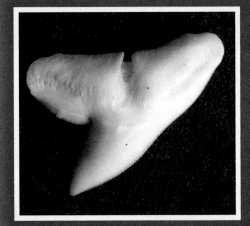

very sharp teeth

The hammerhead shark is a fascinating fish!

GLOSSARY

cartilage   a kind of hard tissue that is lighter than bone

fin   the pointy parts of the shark's body that help it steer

gills   slits in a shark's skin that help it to breathe

prey   an animal that is food for another animal

sensors   black dots on the snout that help the shark to feel signals

skeleton   is made of bones that connect together and give the body shape and protection